the Super...TO
UNDERSTANDING
ANGELS

SHANE WALL

GODLY WRITES PUBLISHING
ORANGEBURG, SC

Published by:
Godly Writes Publishing
P. O. Box 2005
Orangeburg SC 29116-2005

Unless otherwise noted, Scripture quotations are taken from the Amplified® Bible, Copyright © 1954, 1958, 1962, 1964, 1965, 1987 by The Lockman Foundation
Used by permission. www.lockman.org

Scripture quotations marked KJV are taken from the King James Version of the Bible.
Public Domain.

Take note that the name satan and related names are not capitalized, unless the name begins a sentence. We choose not to acknowledge him, even to the point of violating grammatical rules.

A Supernatural Guide to Understanding Angels
ISBN 10: 0996799761
ISBN 13: 978-0-9967997-6-8

Cover design by David C. Marshall, Jr.

For Worldwide Distribution. Printed in the U.S.A.

www.shanewall.com

TABLE OF CONTENTS

FOREWORD

Today's movies, plays and books bombard us with images of wizards, witches, warlocks, vampires and werewolves. A casual observer would believe that the supernatural has only to do with the dark side. Pastor Shane Wall, however, lays out the case that God created and is in charge of everything both seen and unseen and gives access to the unseen realm to whomever He chooses. Our Father has allowed Pastor Wall to view the hidden world of angelic beings since childhood. In this work, he explains how all of us have the potential to experience the supernatural through the Holy Spirit.

Jesus Himself told us in Luke 11:13 that we only need to ask our Father for His Spirit.

> *"If you then, being evil, know how to give good gifts to your children, how much more will your heavenly Father give the Holy Spirit to those who ask him?"*
>
> Luke 11:13 (KJV)

Pastor Wall points out that Satan's followers fervently seek access to the power of the occult world in order to further the cause of their master. Should we not then, as God's children, ardently petition our Father for supernatural knowledge, not to further our own agendas, but to know His will and accomplish His purpose?

Within these pages, Pastor Wall addresses this question and much more. Believers will find this book a practical guide to seeking God, but will also receive insights into why we should want to gain access to the spiritual realms with the proper mindset and motivation.

I believe that this work will be a help to many people desiring a closer relationship with God. The fact that Pastor Wall is clear in saying God is in control and commands the angels will reassure many who are skeptical of literature regarding angelic beings. The book tells us plainly that rather than seeking angelic intervention, we need to seek God Himself, and He will send His angelic ministers.

The times are perfect for Pastor Wall's teaching. People are clearly unsettled right now due to what's going on around them in the world. They need such a message to refocus their attention on the God Who can secure them through whatever is shaking their lives. This is an exciting book!

—Nettie Canada, M.D., M.S.

CHAPTER I
FIRST ENCOUNTERS

There they were. Their faces were relaxed, but their wings were erect, as if standing at attention. One of them held a sword, pointing upward, posing as a warrior ready for a fight. The angels were suspended directly above Robert, one of my classmates in Mrs. Bering's kindergarten class.

My jaw couldn't have dropped any further, so I closed my mouth and looked around to see if anyone else saw this holy being who glowed with the warmth and breath of God Himself. Melissa was coloring, Jean was getting a tissue, and Kathy was crying because Kendrick wouldn't stop picking on her.

I looked back at the angels, still hovering over my friend Robert. He was busy coloring too, unaware of the wonder happening above him. I blinked twice, three times. The angels were still there, the gaze of the tallest intently locked onto mine.

I found out later that my experience with the angels was to build my faith, but they had also come to protect my classmate Robert's family. After that day, in fact, I never saw Robert again. My teacher told us soon after that Robert's family had moved urgently out of town. I could only imagine what the family was going through, something so critical that angels had to protect even the kindergartner before he left the city.

That was my first experience in seeing angels with my natural eyes and my introduction to discerning beings in the realm of the spirit. While my encounter was peaceful, the first time someone engaged with an angel in the Bible was under much more intense circumstances.

In the book of Genesis, God promised Abram that he and his wife, Sarai, would bear a son. Sarai grew tired of waiting, so she concocted a plan that Abram would have a child by her Egyptian maid, Hagar.

After Hagar conceived, Sarai, renamed Sarah, became enraged and jealous and began treating Hagar harshly.

Because of the bitter treatment, Hagar fled, pregnant with Abram's son. The scripture below introduces the first recorded biblical communication between an angel and a human being.

But the Angel of the Lord found her by a spring of water in the wilderness on the road to Shur.

And He said, Hagar, Sarai's maid, where did you come from, and where are you intending to go? And she said, I am running away from my mistress Sarai.

The Angel of the Lord said to her, Go back to your mistress and [humbly] submit to her control.

Also the Angel of the Lord said to her, I will multiply your descendants exceedingly, so that they shall not be numbered for multitude.

Genesis 16:7-10 (AMP)

This initial *first* angelic encounter in the Bible delivers a significant revelation as to the purpose of angels on the Earth. Popular lore seems to suggest that angels happen upon people at random times, but these instances are never random. Angels follow God's orders to arrive at a specific location at a specific time, and only to carry out God's specific purpose.

main

We don't command angels, but rather God instructs and commands them according to His will. When we hear or read about the activities of angels, we are literally witnessing the will of God unfolding in the lives of those whom the angels are helping. Having said that, I will note further that our hope should never be aimed at seeing angels perform any task that God has not commanded.

Angels, just like any other creation of God, are designed to bring Him praise, honor and glory. While the thought of seeing or interacting with angels may be exciting, remember that the focus of the supernatural is always to bring you closer to Jesus.

Most Bible scholars believe and attest that the *Angel of the Lord* Who spoke with Hagar in the scripture above is Jesus Christ, the coming Messiah, centuries before being conceived as a human, in the womb of Mary. This is my belief as well.

Even though this is Jesus, He is still referred to as *Angel* in this scripture because the time of His full manifestation had not yet come. Jesus' appearance in angelic form lets us know that our journey in understanding the supernatural is all about Him.

Going further into our study of angels, we will next explore the three different types of angels that are revealed to us in the Bible. Each type of angel is assigned specific tasks in order to perfectly carry out God's will.

CHAPTER II
TYPES AND PURPOSES OF ANGELS

"You never know when an angel will show up in my house. It happens when you least expect it," I told Connie, my girlfriend at the time. From the look on her face, I could tell that she didn't believe me. I still remember her rolling her eyes.

A couple of weeks later, we were at the house watching a movie. I think it was Sherlock, because she loved mysteries. I was drawn into the movie, but Connie kept taking furtive glances down the hallway. "I thought you said we were here alone," Connie said. I frowned, confused. "Shane, I just saw someone in the hallway go from one room to the other." She grabbed my arm, her voice rising higher with every word.

"Connie, I told you that I have angels in my..."

Before I could finish my sentence, she leaped from the couch and scrambled her way to the front door. I tried to hold in my laughter, but it was just too funny—you should've seen the look on her face.

After witnessing Connie's expression, I can easily imagine how people in the Bible reacted when they saw an angel for the first time. Reading scripture, we get the impression that angels know their presence can be startling, as they often reassured those who were alarmed by saying, "Do not be afraid." God revealed to me that the angel Connie saw was one of the guardian angels who protects my family and our home, but I'll share more about that later. I believe that God's purpose for making the angel visible to Connie was to strengthen her faith in Him, and it did, although her first reaction was one of fright.

In fact, God has a purpose for every angel. The Bible groups angels into three orders, or categories: seraphim, archangels and cherubim. Each group of angels has specific duties, assigned to them by God.

Seraphim

In the year that King Uzziah died,
[in a vision] I saw the Lord sitting

> *upon a throne, high and lifted up,*
> *and the skirts of His train filled the*
> *[most holy part of the] temple.*
>
> *Above Him stood the seraphim;*
> *each had six wings: with two [each]*
> *covered his [own] face, and with two*
> *[each] covered his feet, and with two*
> *[each] flew.*
>
> *Then flew one of the seraphim*
> *[heavenly beings] to me, having a*
> *live coal in his hand which he had*
> *taken with tongs from off the altar;*
>
> Isaiah 6:1&2,6 (AMP)

According to Isaiah, the seraphim are situated close to where God is seated on His throne, and this specific order of angels is only referenced in two verses of the entire Bible. The Hebraic translation of the term *seraphim* speaks of the angels' appearance being as lightning and fiery, their six wings revealing the majesty of God's holiness.

Since they are in close proximity to God, two of their wings cover their faces because they're not worthy to look upon His holiness. The two wings that cover their feet are symbolic of their walk or ways not being worthy of His actual presence, and their using the final two wings to fly indicates that's how they rejoice and move about to do the bidding of the Almighty.

I have myself experienced the presence of an angel whom the Holy Spirit told me "...came directly from the presence of God." I sensed the unmistakable glory of the Lord emanating from the angel like soothing heat radiating from the sun at the beach. Can you imagine experiencing God's glory from the presence of a seraphim angel who has come directly from the throne room?

Isaiah felt the great power of the seraphim, whose voices shook the doorposts and the thresholds, and filled the temple with smoke. He then felt the great weight of his own imperfections—but a saraph (singular for seraphim) brought Isaiah a burning coal from God's altar, touched his lips with it, and removed the man's sin. After that, Isaiah felt ready to undertake the mission now given him directly by God.

In the next chapter, I'm going to share more about the fact that when we have visions, we are actually seeing into the spiritual realm. But first, let's discover the archangel.

Archangel

> *But when [even] the archangel Michael, contending with the devil, judicially argued (disputed) about the body of Moses, he dared not [presume to] bring an abusive condemnation against him, but [simply] said, The Lord rebuke you!*
>
> Jude 1:9 (AMP)

The term *archangel* doesn't appear in the Old Testament. Even though the term is mentioned in Scripture, no explicit descriptions of the archangel are given. I have, however, had the pleasure of personally seeing the archangel Michael at close proximity.

The archangel Michael is between nine and ten feet tall, and he is cloaked in a dazzlingly white robe. Carefully placed on the robe are blue tassel-like cords that fall down each of his broad shoulders, and he wears a corded belt of the same color. His stance is as solid as a rock, showing he bears the desire and the responsibility to be unflinchingly focused on God and His will. In the times I've seen Michael, he's always looking upward, toward heaven, with an expression of sincere devotion and strict attention to God.

Jude's account of the archangel Michael reveals a heated discussion between him and the devil, satan. Michael and satan are the exact opposites in terms of purpose and creation.

Most people view satan as God's chief competition. But this couldn't be further from the truth. Because satan is a created being, no way could he be in competition with Almighty God. The archangel Michael, another created being, would be considered satan's competition.

Cherubim

Cherubim are the most mentioned of all the angels in the Bible. From near the beginning of human existence, cherubim have played important roles in God's plan. Yet eyewitness accounts of this type of angel today are virtually nonexistent.

Ezekiel, a mighty prophet of the Old Testament, had an amazing experience with God in which he experienced cherubim in the spirit realm.

> *But each one had four faces and*
> *each one had four wings.*
> *And their legs were straight legs,*
> *and the sole of their feet was like the*

*sole of a calf's foot, and they sparkled
like burnished bronze.*

*And they had the hands of a man
under their wings on their four sides.
And the four of them had their faces
and their wings thus:*

*Their wings touched one another;
they turned not when they went but
went every one straight forward.*

*As for the likeness of their faces,
they each had the face of a man [in
front], and each had the face of a
lion on the right side and the face of
an ox on the left side; the four also
had the face of an eagle [at the back
of their heads].*

Ezekiel 1:6-10 (AMP)

His depiction is incredible. He describes the cherubim as having four faces: the face of a man, the face of a lion, the face of an ox, and the face of an eagle.

It's interesting to note that God already had created the cherubim beings before He created mankind. Therefore, who their faces represent existed before those represented were even born. The makeup of the cherubim lets us know that God has had you and me in His heart before the beginning of time.

The cheribums are packed with even more revelation, coupled with what God told Moses and Aaron concerning the tribes of Israel.

> *The Lord said to Moses and Aaron:*
> *The Israelites shall encamp, each by his own [tribal] standard or banner with the ensign of his father's house, opposite the Tent of Meeting and facing it on every side.*
>
> Numbers 2:1&2 (AMP)

God told Moses and Aaron to tell each of the children of Israel to create a banner displaying a symbol of his patriarchal heritage. The illustration of Judah's banner was characterized by a lion, while Reuben's banner displayed the figure of a man. On Ephraim's standard was an ox, and on Dan's was an eagle. From Ezekiel's account we see that the cherubim had four faces but one head, symbolizing that God was the Head of each of the tribes.

Today, we are all God's people, coming from all walks of life, united under one Spirit and one Head. As the physical characteristics of the cherubim point directly to God, it reminds us that our supernatural journey is not about pursuing spooky experiences, but about getting closer to our Father.

Isn't it praiseworthy and comforting to know that we have angels warring on our behalf who can and do master satan and his angels? With the seraphim, archangels and cherubim set by God as warriors and ministers in His undefeatable Kingdom, we have nothing and no one to fear. We can clearly see God's thoughtful plan to always take care of His own.

CHAPTER III
CAN ANYONE SEE ANGELS?

On a Monday evening, I was nearing the end of an episode of *Law and Order SVU*, eager to see what the outcome would be, when my phone rang. It was Michelle, a member of the church I pastor, someone I considered a close daughter of mine.

"Hey, Dad..." she mumbled, somberly.

"Hey, daughter. What's wrong?" I asked.

"Dad, a friend of mine is in labor with her daughter, and the doctors are afraid that she might lose the baby. Will you please pray for her?"

"Of course I will," I responded and I began at once to pray. "Father, in the mighty and matchless name of Jesus Christ, I speak healing to that..." The answer came in an instant. Right at that moment, the Holy Spirit showed me what was happening. But what I observed was completely stunning, so stunning, in fact, that the bold confidence in my voice softened to just above a whisper.

In the realm of the spirit, I saw an angel robed in shimmering white, his face expressing the seriousness of the moment. He was holding the baby tucked securely under his right arm, and the baby's head rested in the palm of his hand. The baby lay still in his arms, reflecting the glowing shimmer from the angel. Suddenly, the angel's head snapped up, looking toward the heavens. And as if responding to a command, he flapped his wings with great strength and carried the baby away into the distance.

As the angel disappeared, I heard a voice—a familiar, very comforting voice. Yes, it was the Comforter Himself, the Holy Spirit. He said, "One hour from now." I sighed. (All of this happened in just a few seconds, right when I began praying for the baby.)

Continuing in prayer, I said in a much calmer and heartfelt manner, "...Lord... touch that family now...with Your love...and with Your comfort. It's in Jesus' name that I do pray... Amen." I sighed again.

I couldn't help but sound the way I was feeling. I said, "I saw an angel. Call them back in one hour, and then call me immediately after you speak with them."

Her response echoed the timbre of my voice. "Ok, Dad. I will."

I sat and prayed in tongues, staring blankly at the TV.

My phone rang sixty-one minutes after I'd hung up from Michelle. I answered.

"Michelle?"

"Yeah, Dad..."

I was quiet, waiting for her to continue speaking. Her voice was solemn and reserved. "...the baby didn't make it. She just passed."

"I know, daughter."

"Yeah, I know you do, Dad. When you said that you saw an angel, I kind of figured what was going to happen."

We know that angels are spiritual beings who are visible in the supernatural realm. But it's important for us to note that an angel's presence and activity aren't always confirmed by our seeing them in our physical surroundings. Whether we see them in the visible or just in the invisible realm, their activity is just as potent and effective.

> *For by him were all things created,*
> *that are in heaven, and that are in*
> *earth, visible and invisible, whether*

> *they be thrones, or dominions, or*
> *principalities, or powers: all things*
> *were created by him, and for him:*
> Colossians 1:16 (KJV)

What many people call a *vision* is God revealing to us what's literally happening in the supernatural realm that He created. In a vision, the Holy Spirit simply makes the events visible to our spiritual eyes. Because we all have spiritual eyes, *anyone* can see angels.

Often I used to say that I have a gift of seeing angels, but one day the Holy Spirit told me to stop saying that I have a *"gift."* He explained that I don't have a gift, but rather an ability, and that ability can be taught. He continued to relay to me that anyone can see and otherwise knowingly experience angels in the supernatural realm, and that all we need is the *understanding*.

Understanding itself unlocks usable insight, releasing to us an ability to accurately perceive secrets of the supernatural realm. Daniel, a wise man of the Old Testament, is an example of how understanding gives information that is hidden in the invisible realm.

> *In the third year of Cyrus king of*
> *Persia a thing was revealed unto*

Daniel, whose name was called Belteshazzar; and the thing was true, but the time appointed was long: and he understood the thing, and had understanding of the vision.

Daniel 10:1 (KJV)

Just as God opened Daniel's eyes, He can open yours. Through the revelation God has given me, I can teach anyone to see in the spirit realm. Teaching transfers ability from one person to another. When you learn what I teach, you'll receive the understanding, unlocking your ability to see angels. This teaching is only for the person who's willing to be transformed by the Holy Spirit from perceiving life solely in the natural to being aware of the workings in the spiritual realm.

But the natural man receiveth not the things of the Spirit of God: for they are foolishness unto him: neither can he know them, because they are spiritually discerned.

1 Corinthians 2:14 (KJV)

A key to spiritual discernment is knowing what we have access to. Satan worshippers are fully aware of what they have access to in the spiritual realm. They are able to see far beyond what their natural eyes behold. But tell me something: Why would God grant the enemy opportunities to see more than His children can see?

The answer is that He hasn't. The Lord has made the same depth of sight into the spiritual realm available to us as is to those who study and practice demonic activities.

Most people are convinced that occult practitioners have an upper hand over the spiritual abilities that Christians possess, and many believers tremble in fear before those who claim to be empowered by the kingdom of darkness. Weak faith is widely common in the Christian church because, compared to those who work witchcraft and other dark arts, the majority of Christians fail to display the power that God desires for us to possess and demonstrate unto His glory.

How do workers of dark arts and witchcraft get their abilities to interact with the spiritual realm? They're well taught and well trained, and they use biblical principles to accomplish their furtive deeds.

Satan cannot create, so he pervertedly copies principles that our Father has established. For example, when God created man, He breathed spirit into him, thus creating a law: *Spirits can enter bodies*. Therefore, evil spirits are allowed to enter bodies, in what is known as *demonic possession*.

The enemy has even perverted faithfulness and loyalty. Just as occurs in God's kingdom, Satan requires his followers to spend time in prayer and meditation on written texts in order to access the spirit realm, exactly the way God requires us to spend time with Him and meditate on His Word.

For any human to advance into the spiritual realm, a medium must be used. In God's kingdom, the medium is the Holy Spirit, but in satan's kingdom the mediums are demonic spiritual guides. These mediums issue the sacrificial requirements to the humans who desire to enter into the spiritual realm.

God created the supernatural realm before the earth was ever formed. We think it's spooky, but in the words of Sid Roth, an international minister and host of the television program *It's Supernatural*, living a life that's *naturally supernatural* is the life all Christians should experience daily.

Why are Christians so far behind in experiencing the supernatural realm, compared to those who are demonically influenced? Those interested in satanic access and operation in the spiritual realm invest a lot of time and personal energy into fulfilling their passion. How many Christians are passionate about spending hours in prayer daily and reading God's Word as if it is the only life-giving source on the planet? How many regard fasting each week as a means of weakening the flesh so that, coupled with prayer, their spirit will be sensitive to the Holy Ghost?

Nobody balks at the fact that witches and warlocks take their students through rigorous training before performing evil deeds assigned to them. On the contrary, people accuse pastors who train their members how to see, hear and operate in the supernatural realm of teaching deceptive practices.

While some giftings of the Holy Spirit cannot be imparted through teaching, seeing angels is not a gift. It is a capability that God is pleased to permit by His Holy Spirit. In the next chapter, I'll teach you how God's Word guides us into the wonderful experience of living life in the supernatural realm, just as our Lord did.

Jesus went away and prayed many times, but what happened during his times of prayer was never recorded. Those are the supernatural times that we will experience. We should not expect to experience the supernatural in public display of God's power if we're not experiencing His glorious realm during our private time with Him.

> *Then answered Jesus and said unto*
> *them, Verily, verily, I say unto you,*
> *The Son can do nothing of himself,*
> *but what he seeth the Father do: for*
> *what things soever he doeth, these*
> *also doeth the Son likewise.*
>
> John 5:19 (KJV)

In the verse above, Jesus states that He only does what He sees His Father do. How did Jesus see God's activities? During prayer, Jesus could see what was happening in the spiritual realm. Whatever He saw God doing, He knew that He was to emulate those actions. Therefore, when we pray, we can receive visions, see angelic beings, and hear the clear and audible voice of the Holy Spirit.

These and other experiences reveal God's will that He wants executed in our lives. Just like our Lord, we can see what our Father is doing in prayer and imitate everything that He does.

CHAPTER IV
SEEING THE INVISIBLE

I don't have office visits before I minister Sunday mornings at the church I pastor, but a few Sundays ago was different. As I opened the door to my office, the sight was glorious! Two angels were suspended near the 12-foot ceiling in the two corners above my office door. They were dressed in shimmering white robes and had their hands folded in front of them. Two of my spiritual sons who were there couldn't see them, but they could definitely sense the angels' majestic presence.

Despite my awe at their appearance, with them glowing like a full moon in a cloudless sky, what really held my attention was their facial expressions. Both of them looked directly at me. Their countenances displayed such gratifying pleasure, as that of a father seeing his first child being born.

After a couple of minutes passed, I looked back at them. They were still gazing at me, as if they knew something was going to happen that was unknown to me, as though they had planned my surprise birthday party.

I deduced their presence and demeanor meant that our Sunday morning worship service would be remarkably powerful that day—and it was. God gave me astonishing revelations from the list of scriptures I'd studied—revelations that were received by me in the middle of ministering. I was utterly amazed at the obvious joy on the faces of the congregants, as many of them whipped out their phones to take pictures of the scriptures displayed on the projection walls and to write down notes about what I was teaching.

As I often do after delivering the message, I asked my assistant pastor to minister in the gifts of the Spirit. The atmosphere radiated with power! People were unashamedly reaching and crying out to God as if they were privileged to worship Him right in front of His throne. The intense adoration for the Lord was unmistakably pleasing to Him, as His unhindered presence permeated even the very air we breathed. People were healed from years of inner pain, mental anguish, unforgiveness and chronic worry.

One of the testimonies resulting from that service came from a member who shared that he was quick to get angry, but he now experiences a settled spirit. He's enjoying peace beyond his imagination. He said he still can't believe how calm he is, even during the most trying situations.

As I reflect back on that Sunday morning, I ask myself, "Did the angels say anything to me while they were in the office?" No, they did not, neither did they display any noticeable body movements. They were just there, suspended in the air, and even though their lips were together, their smiling faces exhibited a brilliance unmatched by that of any human I've ever seen.

Many of us are accustomed to regarding the facial expressions of our family and friends as indicators of their true feelings. That particular day, the glorious appearance of the faces of those angels was sign enough to me to expect and know that God had planned something remarkable for His people in that service.

Even with the overwhelming radiance that was bestowed on the angels, they weren't made visible to the naked eye, and they didn't have to be. The reality of what's visible only in the realm of the spirit, isn't dependant upon what is perceived by our natural senses. The unseen world is more real than what we can see, because everything we see in the natural is temporary. What we don't see in the physical is everlasting. Interesting, right? It's pretty contradictory to conventional thinking. But here's the proof:

> *Since we consider and look not to the things that are seen but to the things that are unseen; for the things that are visible are temporal (brief and fleeting), but the things that are invisible are deathless and everlasting.*
>
> 2 Corinthians 4:18 (AMP)

What we're observing in the natural can be so very distracting from what we should be observing in the supernatural. As the Holy Spirit has personally taught me, I'll teach you now how He opens our spiritual eyes to see what God wants to reveal to us.

Our attitude determines what we see, and perception is everything. Why do you want to encounter angels and other activity in the spirit realm? Also, why do you think God wants *you*, specifically, to have such experiences?

The reason *why* we desire greater sensitivity to the spiritual realm will affect whether God will allow it or not. God has only one purpose for showing us what's in the supernatural realm. To reveal His will. The Holy Spirit only wants us to desire seeing the invisible so that we can better know God's will and respond accordingly. Without a heart to please the Father, seeing what God sees is virtually needless in our lives.

> *So Jesus answered them by saying, I assure you, most solemnly I tell you, the Son is able to do nothing of Himself (of His own accord); but He is able to do only what He sees the Father doing, for whatever the Father does is what the Son does in the same way [in His turn].*
>
> John 5:19 (AMP)

Jesus boldly declared that He only did what He saw His Father doing, and we have to do the same. For me, the Holy Spirit shows me a vision of myself doing something in particular, and I know at an instant that what I'm seeing in the Spirit is exactly what God desires for me to do. Our heavenly Father will show us the supernatural realm by His Holy Spirit, so we can do exactly what He wants us to do.

Often when I minister, I see angels lined up shoulder to shoulder in the back of the sanctuary. They stand at attention while I'm preaching, but at a certain point, usually near the end of my message, they begin to flap their wings violently, lifting their knees intermittently, as if to run in place in no particular rhythm. The Holy Spirit explained to me that when that happens, He's ready for me to begin ministering deliverance to the people in the service. Hence, I know what to do because of what I see in the Spirit.

One of the most important statements I can ever make concerning seeing in the Spirit is this: "I only want to see what God wants to show me." So many people think that experiencing the realm of the supernatural is spooky and weird, so they set their hearts and minds to begin focusing on and expecting bizarre and strange spiritual sights and experiences. God greatly desires for us to grow deeper in Him, but we must be careful to only desire to see and encounter whatever He wants to show us.

God is sovereign. He shows us whatever *He* wants us to know and He does that *when* He wants us to know it. We cannot force God's power to use our senses, even if we sincerely want to help someone other than ourselves. Our Father is not moved by fear when we face a situation.

He will say or show us only what is absolutely necessary for us to know.

We don't have to "try to see in the spirit realm." God knows exactly where our spiritual eyes are, and He will present the spirit realm to us right where we can't miss it. As we invest time in prayer, fasting and in God's Word, and when the Holy Spirit wills, our natural or spiritual senses will meet the dimension of the supernatural head on. We must always be satisfied with every spiritual experience God gives us, or else we'll begin to create false visions in our minds and destroy the purity and validity of our experience.

> *And God sent an angel unto Jerusalem to destroy it: and as he was destroying, the Lord beheld, and he repented him of the evil, and said to the angel that destroyed, It is enough, stay now thine hand. And the angel of the Lord stood by the threshingfloor of Ornan the Jebusite.*
>
> *And David lifted up his eyes, and saw the angel of the Lord stand between the earth and the heaven, having a drawn sword in his hand*

stretched out over Jerusalem. Then
David and the elders of Israel, who
were clothed in sackcloth, fell upon
their faces.

1 Chronicles 21:15-16 (KJV)

When it's actually God revealing an occurrence in the invisible world to us, there will be an instinctive response from our spirit, just as David reacted to what God showed him in the verse above. If we consciously form imaginations, trying to fool ourselves that what we're seeing is real, not only will there be no truth to what we've seen, there will also be no truth in our pretense of a response. God gives us this ability for the express purpose of firmly grasping His will so that we can complete our assignments. In the following verse we see how Jacob came to know God's will through the presence of angels and God's direct Word to him.

And he dreamed, and behold a
ladder set up on the earth, and the
top of it reached to heaven: and
behold the angels of God ascending
and descending on it.

And, behold, the Lord stood above it, and said, I am the Lord God of Abraham thy father, and the God of Isaac: the land whereon thou liest, to thee will I give it, and to thy seed;

And thy seed shall be as the dust of the earth, and thou shalt spread abroad to the west, and to the east, and to the north, and to the south: and in thee and in thy seed shall all the families of the earth be blessed.

And, behold, I am with thee, and will keep thee in all places whither thou goest, and will bring thee again into this land; for I will not leave thee, until I have done that which I have spoken to thee of.

And Jacob awaked out of his sleep, and he said, Surely the Lord is in this place; and I knew it not.

Genesis 28:12-16 (KJV)

Whether we're conscious or asleep, seeing angels is usually a sign that a part of God's will is about to be revealed to us, though we are never to assume an interpretation of what we see or hear in the spirit realm. Even if God only reveals a small part of an entire scene, we shouldn't use our imagination to fill in the gaps of what we've experienced. If the Holy Spirit seems to be less than forthcoming with the interpretation, rest in the fact that He knows when we need to receive and proclaim what God is revealing. If we assume anything else, we're leaning to our own understanding, instead of God's understanding.

Now that we have the correct intentions for seeing in the Spirit, let's unlock how to see into the spiritual realm:

- Know that God desires to show you happenings in the supernatural realm
- Live a consecrated life by praying, fasting, living the Scriptures you read, and being free from sin
- Maintain a conscious attitude to only want God's will to be done, no matter what that may be
- Pray sincerely for specific people or groups of people
- Tell the Holy Spirit that you want Him to interrupt you anytime He needs you

- Pray in tongues throughout the day, even if it's in a whisper
- Always seek God's understanding for whatever happens in your life
- Realize that prayer is not a speech. It's a conversation. Give the Holy Spirit ample time in prayer to respond to you... by Word or by vision
- Allow only the fruit of the Spirit to be your every response to life (Galatians 5:22&23)
- Interview every thought before pondering on it, according to Philippians 4:8

(I have more in-depth reading on each of these points on my website at shanewall.com/angels.)

These are the keys that can activate your senses to the realm of the spirit. These keys should not be events in your life, but rather your lifestyle as a supernatural child of God.

It seems too simple, doesn't it? The reality of being sensitive to the spirit realm can actually be attributed to God seeing that you have the right heart attitude before He reveals His divine purpose to you.

Of course, I could give you a regimen of praying every day for two hours, fasting every week for 48 hours and reading at least 12 chapters of the Bible a day. Sure, it would make you *feel* more spiritual and more worthy to have God give you phenomenal experiences in the Spirit. But God doesn't look at the outward show of religiosity; He looks at the intent of the heart that wants nothing more than His will to be done. That individual not only gets God's attention, but is also favored to have God reveal His secrets.

Seeing in the Spirit realm is a privilege in any Christian's life, but the reality is that God strongly desires for us to see His will, which was formerly hidden from our understanding, carried out based on what He has revealed to us. This is what causes the supernatural engineering that's used to create what will soon be visible in the physical realm. When we know God's will, we can fulfill it to the greatest extent. This method may seem too good to be true to work as well as I claim it will, but God has never despised nor rejected a heart that is humbled to say, "Not my will, but Thy will be done."

> *The sacrifices of God are a broken*
> *spirit: a broken and a contrite heart,*
> *O God, thou wilt not despise.*
>
> Psalm 51:17 (KJV)

CHAPTER V
OTHER ANGELIC ENCOUNTERS

Seeing in the spiritual realm doesn't happen around the clock, nor can it be turned on and off like a light switch. The Holy Spirit gives us access into the invisible world so that we can better know God's will, His timing and His purpose for every matter and situation under the sun—at the specific moment that He wants to reveal that information.

Don't be discouraged if you haven't had a supernatural encounter in an entire day, week or month. The focus of our Christian walk should always be to please the Father, as Jesus taught us. It pleases God for us to commune with Him, and He uses our prayers, our times of fasting and our overall consecration to show us and speak to us about every situation we face. Prayer, fasting and living the Word of God are all powerful supernatural experiences, done on Earth, but also affect the heavenly realm.

I have had many angelic encounters in my life, but nowhere near the number of personal encounters that I've had with the Holy Spirit in prayer. I want you to be encouraged to know, however, that the supernatural realm is real and available to you, by sharing a few more encounters that I've had with angels to further develop your understanding of their character, their inclusion and their purpose in our lives.

Running Angels

I'm a big fan of praying in tongues on the way to a service where I'm going to be preaching. As I was driving, I closed my eyes for two seconds, in response to a touch that the Holy Spirit bestowed upon me. When I opened my eyes, they widened as I saw two angels running in front of my car, and an angel running along each side of my car.

Their presence and the energy they exerted caused me to think of God's gracious love, passionate care and vigilant protection of me, bringing me to tears. I was so moved by their presence that I felt as if I were on the set of a movie, with the angels' bright garments and majestic statues surrounding me in a wisp of air. I seemed to be experiencing cinematic [*motion picture*] special effects in real life. As the angels ran, I continued to pray in tongues, worshipping God, my Lord.

I found out later that I was honored with the angels' presence because this was to be the service when I would begin teaching a series called *The Spirit of Man*. I knew that this series would open the hearts of the congregants to realize who God, in His power and authority, has caused them to be. They were about to learn their identities as children of God and why their spirits are important enough for Him to feed and nurture them.

I don't even remember when the angels left my car as I traveled, but I do vividly recall that their presence let me know how crucial [*important*] this sermon series would be. Many times, the appearance of angels shows the importance of what we are carrying, much as when Mary was told by an angel that she would be impregnated by the Holy Spirit, bearing a child whose name was to be Jesus.

Be assured that whatever gift God has given you in ministry, or whatever you're carrying for God's glory, is well protected. His angels are always on assignments of ministry and protection.

Warrior in the Locker Room

About to hurry to my next class amid a sea of high school kids, I stopped at my gym locker. My locker visit was never complete without someone calling out behind me, "Hey, Jesus Junior!" Even during my high school years, I was very serious about ministry, often carrying a small, orange Bible with me everywhere.

Little did I know that I would experience the presence of an angel, right in my gym class. As I was packing up my gym clothes in the locker room, I heard an angry voice behind me. "Hey, Jesus Junior," someone snarled. "Stop talking about Jesus so much to everybody!" I turned around to see K.C. hovering over me, a knife in one hand threatening to slice me open, his other hand coiled in a fist.

The locker room went quiet, and everyone froze, looking at the knife that K.C. clutched. I froze too, not knowing what to do. Suddenly, the Holy Spirit whispered instructions to me. When I heard His voice, I received immediate strength and courage in my young heart. I turned, got the Bible out of the locker, faced my classmate and the knife. Following the Holy Spirit's further instructions, I threw the Bible on the floor between him and me, pointed at the Bible, and yelled defiantly, "CROSS IT!"

Startled, K.C. looked at the Bible, looked at me, then breathed in sharply as his jaw dropped to the floor. *He couldn't possibly be so scared of me*, I thought. I spun around and looked up, and there he was, a warrior angel towering over me and K.C., his wings expanded to their fullest, and with an outraged expression on his face, ready to attack. I later found out that only K.C. and I saw the warrior angel. Stepping back, K.C. ran out of the locker room faster than greased lightning. He didn't return to school for the next three weeks.

As I reflect on that day, I always remember how God Himself sent reinforcements to my rescue. I hadn't always been a perfect son to Him. I probably could have spent more time in prayer the week before. But for my Heavenly Father to deem me precious enough for Him to lift His finger to dispatch one of His strong and majestic angels to my rescue was enough to bring me to my knees.

In that locker room, with a knife threatening to end my life, I was rescued by one of God's angels, a certain sign of His love, care and protection that follows me wherever I go. As a citizen of the Kingdom of God, you too have the benefit of being protected by His angels. Remember that God loves you, His precious and wonderful child, and He's there to protect you from the wiles of the enemy, even as they plot against you to steal, kill and destroy.

Getting a glimpse of the angels who guard us is an amazing experience, but there's nothing like seeing an angel minister to people in an audience. On more occasions than I can count, I've watched angels fly into services where I was ministering. After I've delivered the sermon, they often have hovered in the sanctuary, around three feet above the people.

Frequently, they're carrying satchels appearing to be made of raw tan leather. On the Holy Spirit's cue, they begin pouring out a golden, oil-like substance that literally goes inside of the people. It never fails that the same individuals who have this liquid poured inside of them immediately respond by intensely raising their level of worship and praise, with tears often accompanying their reaction to this supernatural, personal ministry by the angels.

I have also experienced angels suspended above people in church services while I'm teaching. An angel would fly to certain individuals, touch them, and fly back to their suspended position near the ceiling, on alert for another command.

The Holy Spirit told me that this interaction occurs for those who prayed in their hearts while hearing the Word being taught. "Their faith touched God," He said to me. I've learned in my personal relationship with God that anytime we say something that touches God, He'll respond by touching us back. This touch delivers the answer we requested after hearing His Word.

Angels in a Car

As a teenage driver, I had somewhat of a heavy foot. I would break the speed limit on every street, highway, freeway, alley and roundabout that you can think of.

One day, I was running late for work, speeding down the road, when an old model car pulled out slowly in front of me, going ten miles under the limit. I threw my hand up angrily and tried to pass the vehicle for at least two miles, checking my watch, revving the engine, and swerving back and forth in my lane.

Finally, the cars stopped coming, and even though double yellow lines warned me not to, I zipped past the car, giving the elderly couple in the front seat a menacing glance as I pumped the accelerator. As soon as I got in front of them, I looked back, and the car had literally vanished. I checked my mirrors and turned my head to find them because they had no side street to turn off onto. They were driving so slowly, and I cut in front of them so fast, that I couldn't have missed them, but they were gone.

I sped on my way to work, but began to slow down at a site about a mile from where I passed that slow-moving car. A police vehicle was just approaching the scene of a horrible accident that had occurred moments before. Two women were on the side of the road crying, looking in the passenger-side window at an unconscious woman trapped inside a car.

As I slowly passed the scene, looking at bloodstains on the windshield of one of the cars involved, it occurred to me that I could have been in that accident had that old model car not hindered my speed. The Holy Spirit said to me that the elderly couple in the old model car were angels, and they were sent so that I could avoid the coming accident ahead. My heart sank. I wanted to pull over on the side of the road and cry my heart out to God for my being so selfish and mean to those angels who were only trying to protect me.

> Be not forgetful to entertain strangers: for thereby some have entertained angels unawares.
>
> Hebrews 13:2 (KJV)

Angels have the ability to transform themselves into human-like entities. God allows them to do this because he needs human interaction to help protect, instruct and even warn His children of danger or other undesirable circumstances. How often have we encountered strangers who have been kind to us, or who have slowed us down on the highway, and we felt that it was okay to treat them however we wanted at the moment? Don't forget that they could be angels, sent by our loving God to love us, help us, warn us and move us out of harm's way.

Because angels could be "undercover" in the paths of our lives at any time, we may never know who God has sent to assist us. All we can do is to obey Jesus by loving everybody everywhere, and treating others as we would want to be treated. Because you just might be interacting with an angel who has come to assist you.

SOMETHING MORE

In the Bible, we see many examples of angels speaking directly to humans. But why don't they speak to us today the way they spoke to Hagar, Daniel and Mary? The angels I've seen didn't speak to me because they didn't have to. After the infilling of the Holy Spirit in the second chapter of Acts, we see very few instances of angels speaking when they visit, compared to prior visitations in the Old and New Testaments. Even though on rare occasions angels do speak to people, Jesus sent the Holy Spirit to commune with us. Nonetheless, the presence of God's angels are still an active part our lives in the Kingdom of God on Earth.

When I see angelic activity, the Holy Spirit is the One who interprets their actions and reveals their message to me. During my radio interview with Sid Roth, an international minister and host of the television program It's Supernatural, he inquired about angels. He asked, "When you see the angels...could you describe the way one might look?" I'm glad he asked, because I saw an angel appear behind him, standing at attention, looking up, his concentration heavenward. The Holy Spirit said to me that the angel was waiting for instructions.

Angels are obedient to whatever God says, and they're commanded to act according to what God tells them to say or do. I know now that he was waiting for God's command to him as to what was about to happen later that afternoon.

After we recorded the program, Sid and I prayed about a situation that involved evicting an evil spirit from the premises of a piece of property. I saw two angels dismantle the situation on the spot. The Holy Spirit later said to me that the angel I saw during the interview was one of the angels used in that instance.

When I returned home, the Lord told me to ask my wife, an accomplished artist, to paint a portrait of what I saw. A few weeks after I presented the painting to Sid, I was studying scriptural references concerning archangels. The Holy Spirit inserted His words into my stream of thought: "The angel that you saw standing behind Sid was the archangel Michael..." I froze. A gripping feeling of awe came over me, my breathing at a standstill.

As if that revelation wasn't enough, the Holy Spirit continued. "...and I'm not finished using him to protect Sid because satan doesn't like the positive effect he's having on converting the Jewish community that he's hated for centuries, nor the Godly influence he has by teaching millions of people about the supernatural realm. Satan wants to keep Christians away from the spirit realm because he wants to rule that territory with his followers..."

The Holy Spirit ended His discourse by saying, "That's why Michael gets involved. He's protecting Sid from what has been sent out against him, but that won't win.

Dr. Shane Wall being interviewed by Sid Roth when the archangel Michael appeared. Artist: Jasmyne Wall

A CALL FROM THE ALTAR

Our Father, I bring all those who have read this book and their needs before You now. You are Jehovah Jireh, our Provider. We expect from You, by faith, knowing that You will meet our needs according to Your riches in the very glory of Your presence.

My Lord Jesus said, "All that the Father giveth me shall come to me; and him that cometh to me I will in no wise cast out." (John 6:37)

Dear Father, as these who have read this book bring You their praise, prayer and supplication, I know You'll answer them according to Your most holy, just and righteous will. I also ask that You increase their understanding of angels and give them glorious encounters with them.

Oh Lord our God, we know that you hear us, and for all of these and other blessings, *we glorify, honor, praise, thank, bless, worship, adore, extol, exalt, magnify and celebrate YOU, asking in the matchless and precious name of Jesus Christ! According to YOUR will, it is done in Jesus' name!*

If you are a sinner, please pray the following prayer and receive Jesus Christ into your life this very moment. He's waiting for you:

Father God, I come before you now in the name of Jesus Christ. I confess that I am a sinner and I want to be saved from my sins. I do not want to continue in this life of sin. Jesus Christ is Your Son and He died for my sins. Father, You raised Him from the dead!

Jesus, I want You! I really need YOU right now and forever! I invite You into my heart right now. I accept You into my heart right now.

Come in and live in me now! I believe that You have come into my heart and life!

Father, all these things I have asked and prayed in the name of Jesus Christ! Thank You for these and all other blessings! I will live for You and You alone! In Jesus Christ's name I pray, Amen!

I AM SAVED!

ABOUT THE AUTHOR

God has given Dr. Shane Wall earth-shattering revelation on a much overlooked Bible topic, Understanding. Dr. Wall has taken the message and his 31-plus years of ministry experience throughout the world and put these in a critically acclaimed book called *Understanding: All Success Attained By It*.

Through Dr. Wall, countless souls have learned to *understand* life's most difficult challenges simply by cultivating their relationships with God. His shepherd-like heart has counseled many through his top ranked podcast, *Hi, Dad!*, and his Gospel CD, *Conversations With God*.

Dr. Wall's sole aim is to impart his passion for God to everyone he encounters. He pastors The Feast of the Lord in Orangeburg, SC, where he; his wife, Jasmyne; and their son, Joshua Elisha, reside.

CONTACT

Shane Wall
P. O. Box 2005
Orangeburg, SC 29116

(803) 395-0190

www.shanewall.com

www.facebook.com/pastorshanewall

www.twitter.com/shane_wall

https://www.linkedin.com/in/shanewall1

OTHER BOOKS BY THE AUTHOR

What Are You Doing After the Dance?
available in print

Understanding: All Success Is Attained By It
print | eBook | audiobook

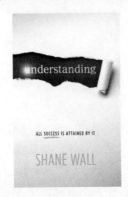